HOMELAND SECURITY
OPERATIONAL ANALYSIS CENTER

Identifying Critical IT Products and Services

SASHA ROMANOSKY, JOHN BORDEAUX, MICHAEL J. D. VERMEER,
JONATHAN W. WELBURN, AARON STRONG, ZEV WINKELMAN

T0059393

Preface

This report documents support by the Homeland Security Operational Analysis Center (HSOAC) for the Critical IT [Information Technology] Products and Services project, which was designed to create a prioritized list of software and businesses that provide IT products and services and, to the extent possible, list the specific IT products whose compromise could have a significant regional or national impact. In addition, we sought to develop a framework that could continue and extend this analysis into the future to accommodate emerging technologies and the evolution of the technology market.

In the past 20 years, the U.S. government, championed by the U.S. Department of Homeland Security (DHS) and in collaboration with other public and private entities, has made considerable progress enumerating the country's critical infrastructure components and National Critical Functions. However, although these efforts have highlighted important sectors and companies that make up the country's critical infrastructure, they have not enabled specific identification of the most-critical computing systems within these networks. Further, multiple methods to assess different kinds of risk might be needed. Examination and enumeration of businesses that provide the most-critical IT products and services will enable DHS and other federal and private-sector elements to better apply a risk-based approach to protecting the country's most-important assets and systems.

This research was sponsored by the National Risk Management Center and conducted within the Strategy, Policy, and Operations Program of the HSOAC federally funded research and development center (FFRDC).

About the Homeland Security Operational Analysis Center

The Homeland Security Act of 2002 (Section 305 of Public Law 107-296, as codified at 6 U.S.C. § 185) authorizes the Secretary of Homeland Security, acting through the Under Secretary for Science and Technology, to establish one or more FFRDCs to provide independent analysis of homeland security issues. The RAND Corporation operates HSOAC as an FFRDC for DHS under contract HSHQDC-16-D-00007.

The HSOAC FFRDC provides the government with independent and objective analyses and advice in core areas important to the department in support of policy development, decisionmaking, alternative approaches, and new ideas on issues of significance. The HSOAC FFRDC also works with and supports other federal, state, local, tribal, and public- and private-sector organizations that make up the homeland security enterprise. The HSOAC FFRDC's research is undertaken by mutual consent with DHS and is organized as a set of discrete tasks. This report presents the results of research and analysis conducted under task order 70RCSA20FR0000060, Identifying Companies That Provide Critical IT Products and Services.

The results presented in this report do not necessarily reflect official DHS opinion or policy.

For more information on HSOAC, see www.rand.org/hsoac. For more information on this publication, see www.rand.org/t/RRA923-2.

Contents

Figures and Tables

Figures

Tables

Summary

In the past 20 years, the U.S. government, championed by the U.S. Department of Homeland Security (DHS) and in collaboration with other public and private entities, has made considerable progress enumerating the country's critical infrastructure components (see, e.g., Executive Order 13636 [Obama, 2013], § 9) and its National Critical Functions (NCFs). However, although these efforts have highlighted important sectors and companies that make up the country's critical infrastructure, they have not enabled specific identification of the most-critical computing systems within these private and public networks.

To help fill that gap, we sought create a prioritized list of software and businesses that provide information technology (IT) products and services and, to the extent possible, to list the specific IT products whose compromise could have a significant regional or national impact. In addition, we sought to develop a framework that could continue and extend this analysis into the future to accommodate emerging technologies and the evolution of the technology market.

Specifically, we examined components of both software risk and business risk. That is, we sought to better understand risks posed by modern networked applications, as well as companies that provide telecommunication and computing business services. In doing so, however, we determined that a *single* prioritization approach—and therefore list of companies or software reflecting an abstracted risk "score"—would obscure the elements that contribute to risks surfaced by our analysis. Instead, we present four distinct lists, each examining various aspects of risk posed to and by IT product and service firms, rather than one comprehensive list of companies as originally envisioned. The work featured four independent workstreams, each producing its own insights to the problem of critical IT products and services:

- We identified and integrated many disparate data sources, in order to identify the most-severe vulnerabilities that have a high likelihood of exploitation and software applications within the U.S. internet protocol space.
- Given the emerging software ecosystem embedded within modern, commercial applications, we collected original data in order to map out the software dependency and ownership structure of the most-referenced libraries.
- We also leveraged existing work to identify specific IT and communication companies that had the greatest measure of business interconnectedness and could potentially suffer the greatest economic loss.
- We developed an original technique for linking NCFs to actual software companies supporting those functions.

Overall, our findings are as follows.

Data that we collected from internet and security companies, together with information security standards, can be used to identify current and evolving software risks. However, an even better understanding of software risk would require additional contextual information about the vulnerabilities that exist, the industries and companies in which they exist, and how the applications support the firms and their operations. Nevertheless, the ability to combine a firm-level inventory of public internet-accessible software, together with severity and exploitability of a vulnerability *at a national scale*, is a capability never previously achieved. We believe that this capability can assist DHS in three important ways:

- First, it provides better guidance for federal agencies on remediation of vulnerabilities on U.S. government networks.
- Next, the U.S. Computer Emergency Readiness Team can leverage it to inform vulnerability and threat reports issued through

the National Cyber Awareness System (see U.S. Computer Emergency Readiness Team, undated a).

- Moreover, when evaluating newly identified (zero-day) vulnerabilities submitted through the federal Vulnerability Equities Process, DHS and other federal agencies can apply an improved understanding of the risks that such vulnerabilities pose to U.S. organizations (see "Vulnerabilities Equities Policy and Process for the United States Government," 2017).

Software supply chains reveal additional dimensions of software risk. To a significant degree, modern commercial applications are built on hundreds of small, distributed free and open-source software libraries owned and maintained in different ways, presenting problems of accountability and foreign control. Therefore, risk assessments can no longer be based simply on application-level analysis because applications (especially web applications) are composed of collections of libraries that have their own risk profiles. Moreover, the landscape of these libraries is constantly changing because libraries are added and updated frequently, making it challenging to quickly assess the implications for risk mitigation. Therefore, in addition to specific vulnerability data, DHS must incorporate open-source software dependencies and ownership into its broader software supply-chain risk framework.

Financial linkages among firms can provide insight into aspects of business risk. Leveraging an existing U.S. Securities and Exchange Commission guideline requiring publicly traded companies to disclose business relationships, as well as recent analytical research, we estimated the total economic loss to an IT or communication firm and its suppliers if the firm experienced an economic shock, such as a cyber incident. In addition, by developing a metric for interconnectedness of business relationships, we were able to identify how smaller yet more-interconnected firms can cause a disproportionately larger impact. The implication of these results for the National Risk Management Center (NRMC) is that they provide objective, defensible insights into potential gaps in the NRMC's understanding of which IT firms might be most critical and why.

The NCF framework can be leveraged to gain insight into the interdependence of critical infrastructure and IT products and services. We present an approach to identify IT firms most relevant to the current articulation of certain NCFs—specifically, those that have been articulated with granularity sufficient to identify assets. Here, we leveraged market analyses to identify firms relevant to specific software market segments by identifying software firms relevant to those assets. The expert judgment required to map software market segments to certain NCFs and assets is straightforward for some functions (e.g., Develop DNS [Domain Name System] Software under the Supply NCF category), while, for others (e.g., the Manage NCF category), additional decomposition to enable identification of relevant assets is required. The NRMC has work underway to decompose NCF statements, which indicates that there is an opportunity to revisit this mapping from market analyses to NCFs once those studies are further along in defining subcomponents and assets of existing NCFs. Nevertheless, for specific areas that might be of high interest to critical infrastructure analysts (e.g., supervisory control and data acquisition, security compliance software, network routing), this work allowed us to develop first-order—unprioritized—lists of firms relevant to several NCFs.

Acknowledgments

We thank our sponsors, Linda Ward and Robert Kolasky, for their support in facilitating and staying engaged throughout the course of the work. We also thank Stefan Haus of the National Infrastructure Simulation and Analysis Center Program Management Office for his assistance in coordinating multiple meetings with stakeholders throughout the National Risk Management Center, and the personnel at several national labs who participated in interviews and in sharing their work with the Homeland Security Operational Analysis Center team. Finally, we would like to thank BitSight and Shodan for data provided for this research.

Within the Homeland Security Operational Analysis Center, we thank Henry H. Willis, director of the Strategy, Policy, and Operations Program, which is the program under which this study was executed. In addition, we benefited at multiple stages of the study from constructive comments from our colleagues Edward Balkovich and Caolionn O'Connell.

Any errors in this report are the responsibility of the authors.

Abbreviations

CII	Core Infrastructure Initiative
CPE	Common Platform Enumeration
CVSS	Common Vulnerability Scoring System
DHS	U.S. Department of Homeland Security
DNS	Domain Name System
EPSS	Exploit Prediction Scoring System
FIRST	Forum of Incident Response and Security Team
FOSS	free and open-source software
IT	information technology
NCF	National Critical Function
NIST	National Institute of Standards and Technology
NVD	National Vulnerability Database
PHP	PHP Hypertext Processor
SCADA	supervisory control and data acquisition

CHAPTER ONE

Introduction

In the past 20 years, the U.S. government, championed by the U.S. Department of Homeland Security (DHS) and in collaboration with other public and private entities, has made considerable progress enumerating the United States' critical infrastructure components and National Critical Functions (NCFs). However, although these efforts have highlighted important sectors and companies that make up the country's critical infrastructure, they have not been able to specifically identify the most-critical computing systems within these networks. For example, Section 9 of Executive Order (EO) 13636 directs DHS to "identify critical infrastructure where a cybersecurity incident could reasonably result in catastrophic regional or national effects on public health or safety, economic security, or national security" (Obama, 2013).[1] However, it also states, "[t]he Secretary shall not identify any commercial information technology products or consumer information technology services under this section" (Obama, 2013). Although the list of critical infrastructure entities has since been created (often referred to as "the Section 9 list"), this one sentence in EO 13636 has prevented a systematic examination of information technology (IT) products and services (such as internet-accessible software) that, if compromised, could result in significant consequences.

A more recent effort by DHS attempts to take a mission assurance (i.e., risk-based) approach to identifying critical IT infrastructure

---

[1] Note that EO 13800 (Trump, 2017) identifies, inter alia, authorities and incentives that the federal government could employ in order to support the cybersecurity risk management of Section 9 entities.

by enumerating the most-important capabilities on which private- and public-sector companies and agencies rely. The NCFs enumerate a list of the 55 functions (see Cybersecurity and Infrastructure Security Agency [CISA], undated). However, even with this approach, a list of critical IT products and services still remains elusive.

With this research, we sought to fill that gap.

Examination and enumeration of the most-critical IT products and services will enable DHS and other U.S. government and private-sector entities to engage with these software developers and development firms and help apply a risk-based approach to protecting the United States' most-important assets and systems.

For this research, we decomposed "IT products and services" into *software risk* and *business risk*. That is, we sought to understand, insofar as was possible, risks posed by modern networked applications and those posed by companies that provide telecommunication and computing business services. This research contained four main approaches: two that address software risk and two that address business risk. In regard to better understanding software risk, we first sought to understand what software was being used throughout U.S. internet space. By knowing which software is most commonly used (and accessible from the public internet), we can then collect more data about the vulnerabilities within those applications and begin to construct a measure of potential risk. In addition, we recognize that modern software applications are built on a foundation of integrated, third-party software libraries (many of which are open source and freely available), so our second approach was to better understand the ecosystem of software library dependencies and the risks associated with these dependencies. We also explored the developer and ownership structures of these libraries in order to better understand who is maintaining the software.

Next, in regard to business risk, we leveraged work by Welburn and Strong, 2021, to understand the total economic loss to both an IT or communication firm and its suppliers if the firm experiences an economic shock, such as a cyberattack, as well as identify firms that are most interconnected with one another, also potentially leading to greater risk. Finally, using the existing list of NCFs, we developed a conceptual approach to connect these functions to firms that manufacture software in support of those functions, thereby potentially identi-fying those firms that most critically support NCFs.

CHAPTER TWO

Software Risk

Understanding software risk requires an understanding of the scope of applications relevant to one's interest, as well as a list of vulnerabilities potentially exposed by those applications. From this initial step, one approach to estimating software risk is to then further characterize those vulnerabilities in order to understand their impact (severity), as well the likelihood that the vulnerability would be exploited. Once this information is known, a decisionmaker can seek to apply more-contextual information about industries, environments, and other criteria, in order to further prioritize remediation or risk-mitigation efforts. This process is illustrated in Figure 2.1.

The figure illustrates this logical flow:

1. Begin with a broad view, considering all applications that might be accessible over the public internet in the United States.[1]
2. Use external data sets to identify the numbers and kinds of vulnerabilities in these applications.
3. Qualify those vulnerabilities in order to identify, then narrow, the set of more-critical vulnerabilities and those that are most likely to be exploited.

Using these steps, we first sought to identify what information was available about the prevalence (use) of networked software

---

[1] *Public internet* refers to applications that can be scanned (i.e., publicly accessible). This excludes the space often referred to as the *deep web*—intranets and applications that are behind firewalls and not scannable from outside their private networks.

Figure 2.1
Improving Awareness of Software Risk

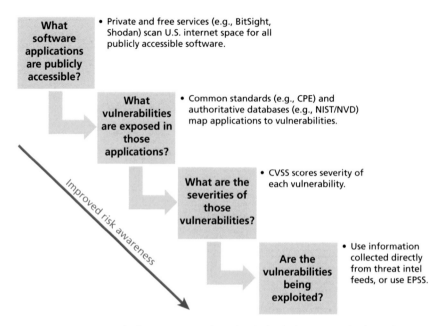

NOTE: CPE = Common Platform Enumeration. CPE is the industry-standard naming scheme to describe vendors, applications, and versions of software and hardware products. See CPE, 2014. NIST = National Institute of Standards and Technology. NVD = National Vulnerability Database. CVSS = Common Vulnerability Scoring System. EPSS = Exploit Prediction Scoring System.

applications,[2] followed by an analysis of known vulnerabilities. We then conducted a complementary analysis in which we further examined the software libraries and dependencies that compose these software applications, noting data-collection and analysis limitations along the way.

---

[2]   Excluded from this analysis are stand-alone, nonnetworked applications, such as many desktop applications.

Software Applications

Internet Application Scanning

To begin the analysis, we collected data from BitSight, a major commercial security company that integrates application fingerprint data into its business services. BitSight, along with its data partners, surveys all routable internet protocol version 4 addresses and more than 300 million host names, across nearly 300 common transmission control protocol and user datagram protocol ports. Responses from running services are then matched against a large database of application fingerprints to identify the software and assign CPE strings.

The complete data set used in this study contains more than 2,700 unique applications and platforms detected across almost 5 million hosts.

Using this information, we next collected the list of all known vulnerabilities potentially exposed by these applications,[3] as recorded by NIST's NVD.[4]

Next, we collected information about the severity (impact) of each vulnerability, as defined by CVSS, the industry standard for assessing the severity of a given software vulnerability.[5] The *severity*, as defined by CVSS, reflects, in part, a measure of impact to the *informa-*

---

[3] Although the application scans reasonably detect or infer the specific products and versions used, they are not always perfectly able to do so. Therefore, in some cases, information collected might be inaccurate. However, we have not identified any systematic measurement errors or biases in the results. Further, we were not able to validate all known vulnerabilities within a particular application because doing so could potentially disrupt or compromise the application itself. Finally, any vulnerabilities included in this analysis represent only those that are publicly known and therefore do not include vulnerabilities known only to the attacker and for which no patches exist (i.e., zero-day vulnerabilities). And so, although omitting zero-day vulnerabilities might lead to an *underestimate* of the true number of vulnerabilities, disclosed but patched vulnerabilities would drive us to *overestimate* the number of vulnerabilities in a given application.

[4] NIST's NVD is an authoritative source of all publicly known software vulnerabilities. See NIST, undated.

[5] CVSS is an industry-standard method of expressing the severity of a software vulnerability. CVSS scores range from 0 (not at all severe) to 10 (critical), and the score is a composite of impact (in terms of confidentiality, integrity, and availability) and other factors that describe the immutable characteristics of the vulnerability. Of course, this represents an aggregate (or

tion system that is compromised, as opposed to a measure of impact to an organization or enterprise overall.

Finally, we collected information about likelihood—or probability that the given vulnerability will be exploited by a malicious actor. Although robust empirical measures of probability have yet to be formally adopted, one effort has begun to develop just such a capability. EPSS was launched in July 2020 as an emerging standard under the governance of FIRST, an international nonprofit organization composed of computer incident response teams from around the world (see FIRST, undated b). EPSS provides a data-driven model to estimate the probability that a given vulnerability will be exploited in the wild within 12 months of being publicly disclosed.

And so, with these data—the list of software applications publicly accessible (collected from application scanning), the associated list of all known vulnerabilities for that software (collected from the NVD), and measures of severity (impact, per CVSS) and probability (per EPSS), we are now able to illustrate one view of software risk, as shown in Figure 2.2.

The lower-left quadrant represents low-severity vulnerabilities that are unlikely to be exploited and can therefore be deprioritized or ignored. Of the approximately 4,700 vulnerabilities represented in this figure, this quadrant reflects almost 2,000 unique vulnerabilities affecting as many as 2.8 billion vulnerable systems.[6] The upper-left quadrant represents nuisance vulnerabilities that, although they are more likely to be exploited, are less severe and might therefore result in only a quick denial of service or information leakage (representing only seven unique vulnerabilities found in up to 42 million installations). The points in the lower right represent a large mass of vulnerabilities to which we refer as a *reservoir of danger*, reflecting the possibility that, if they are exploited, they could become very problematic and require

---

maximum possible) measure of impact that does not account for any specific firm's security posture. See Forum of Incident Response and Security Teams (FIRST), undated a.

[6] These vulnerabilities reflect the complete list of all *potential* vulnerabilities on a given system and might therefore overestimate the true number of actual vulnerabilities exposed by a given application. Identifying the true number of vulnerabilities might not be possible in all cases or might require additional software scanning that could compromise the system.

Figure 2.2
Exploitability Versus Severity, by Asset Count

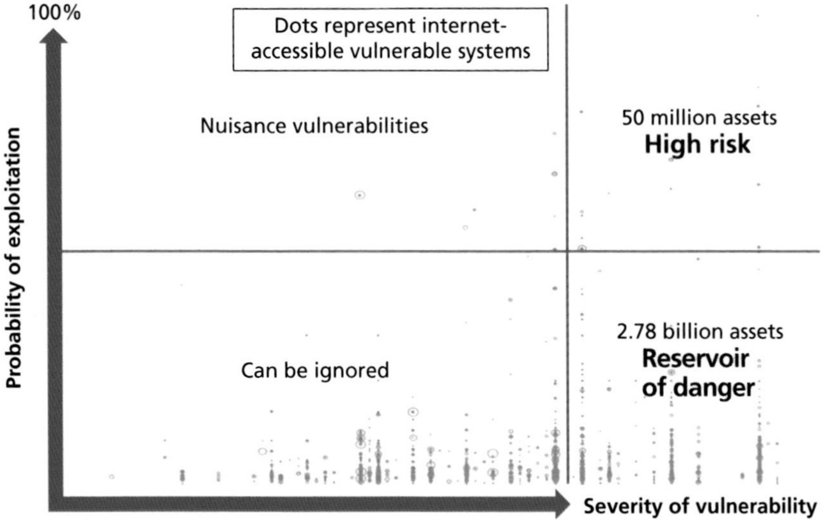

SOURCES: BitSight and NVD data.
NOTE: The vertical axis is a measure of the probability that a vulnerability will be exploited, according to EPSS, and the horizontal axis is a measure of vulnerability severity, according to CVSS. Each point represents groups of vulnerable systems along these dimensions, with some points representing thousands of vulnerable systems, and other larger points representing tens of millions of vulnerable systems. Note that EPSS scores are not available for the complete set of vulnerabilities, so this figure displays results for the 4,700 vulnerabilities for which EPSS scores have been estimated (out of a total of 36,000 unique vulnerabilities). The current EPSS model generated scores for vulnerabilities publicly disclosed between July 2018 and July 2019.

prompt attention (representing almost 2,700 vulnerabilities in as many as 2.8 billion vulnerable systems). Finally, the high-risk vulnerabilities shown in the upper right reflect those vulnerabilities that could possibly lead to a full compromise of a computing system and are more likely to be exploited (reflecting 39 unique vulnerabilities, in up to 50 million vulnerable systems).

The list of the 20 most prevalent high-risk vulnerabilities is shown in Table 2.1 (this represents our first list of potentially risky software or businesses).

Table 2.1
The 20 Most Prevalent High-Risk Vulnerabilities

Vendor	Product Category	CVE
Apache	Web server	CVE-2019-0211
Debian Linux	Operating system	CVE-2018-7602 CVE-2018-16509 CVE-2019-5420 CVE-2018-10900 CVE-2018-10933 CVE-2018-17456 CVE-2019-8942 CVE-2019-0211
WordPress	Web application	CVE-2019-8942
Ruby on Rails	Web application	CVE-2019-5420
Microsoft	Server (Windows Server 2012)	CVE-2018-8544 CVE-2018-8423 CVE-2018-8440
	Server (Windows Server 2008)	CVE-2019-0708 CVE-2018-8544 CVE-2018-8423 CVE-2018-8440
Drupal	Web application	CVE-2018-7602 CVE-2019-6340

Discussion

These results provide very powerful and novel insights into understanding software risk. The ability to associate and visualize vulnerability severity with exploitability has never (to our knowledge) been possible before. The results provided above also suggest that vulnerabilities that lead to greater impact *do not* appear to be much more likely to also be exploited. Although conventional wisdom might lead one to expect attackers to target severer vulnerabilities more often, we show that this is not necessarily the case.

This insight becomes very important for risk management and vulnerability remediation efforts by any organization that needs to prioritize its software patching processes. Whether as an individual company looking to patch its networks or as a federal agency looking to understand national threats, such as with the U.S. Computer Emergency Readiness Team's National Cyber Awareness Program, or when assessing defensive equities from a newly discovered (zero-day) vulnerability as part of the U.S. government's Vulnerability Equities Process. Further, DHS's Binding Operational Directive 19-02 requires patching vulnerabilities with a CVSS score of 10 (i.e., critical) within 15 days.[7] Our results, however, suggest that this guidance can be improved by also considering the exploitability of the given vulnerability.

The previous analysis highlighted a very important consideration when seeking to construct a useful measure of software risk, which is that, although many internet services are stand-alone and static applications (e.g., file transfer protocol, secure shell, database servers), the evolution of the internet has driven web applications, uniquely, to become incredibly complicated and built on a foundation of dozens of web components and plugins. Therefore, we address this limitation in the next section by examining the software libraries and components that are used to build modern software applications.

Software Dependency Component Libraries

The landscape of software applications in the United States is heavily dependent on free and open-source software (FOSS) libraries. Some estimates suggest that more than 80 percent of existing software products use some amount of FOSS, and the use of FOSS has been steadily growing, as has the number of confirmed or suspected breaches related to open-source vulnerabilities (Sonatype, undated). This heavy dependency on FOSS libraries presents a significant potential risk to critical IT products and services, and adequate risk assessment and mitigation requires analysis of open-source software dependency.

Various government and industry efforts, both prior and ongoing, attempt to assess this landscape and provide frameworks for evaluating the risk implications from open-source software dependencies. The National Telecommunications and Information Administration,

---

[7]   See U.S. Computer Emergency Readiness Team, undated b, and "Vulnerabilities Equities Policy and Process for the United States Government," 2017.

a component of the U.S. Department of Commerce, in the course of its work tied to the software supply chain and software component transparency, has been working on creating a framework for a software bill of materials that could create a common framework for evaluating components and vulnerabilities in the software ecosystem (National Telecommunications and Information Administration, undated). Authors of publications from the ongoing NIST effort on vulnerability management have also recommended keeping a "current and complete inventory of the patchable software" installed on devices (Souppaya and Scarfone, 2013, p. 6). One of the primary lessons learned from these and other recent efforts, however, is that the significant and growing complexity of the FOSS landscape, coupled with the lack of a standardized software-naming schema, make it very challenging to address the risk from FOSS in a consistent and comprehensive manner (Nagle et al., 2020).

The FOSS landscape consists of millions of software libraries with branching versions owned and managed by a wide array of different entities, and the complexity of this space is growing each year. Two recent reports, one on the Linux Foundation's Core Infrastructure Initiative (CII) and the other a collaboration between Veracode and the Cyentia Institute (a data analysis and research company), address the state of open-source software libraries (Nagle et al., 2020; Veracode and Cyentia Institute, 2020). In the next section, we describe the CII and Veracode/Cyentia findings in more depth and follow that with our analysis of the implications for critical infrastructure risk.

The Most–Commonly Used Open-Source Software Libraries

Each of these two reports (CII and the Veracode/Cyentia) provides two inventories of the open-source software libraries most commonly used in applications by public and private organizations (one inventory for public and one for private organizations). CII performed its census using data from automated scans and human audits performed by partnering software composition analysis and application security companies, while Veracode and Cyentia used the Veracode scanning platform database. Each published multiple lists of the most-used libraries in its data set. CII described the ten most-common libraries, irrespective of programming language, and a separate list of the ten most-common libraries other than JavaScript libraries. Veracode and Cyentia separated their results into the ten most-common libraries in each of eight programming languages: Go, Java, JavaScript, .NET, PHP Hypertext Processor (PHP), Python, Ruby, and Swift. Their results are shown in Table 2.2. The results from CII overlap significantly with those of Veracode and Cyentia and are not shown.

Table 2.2
The Most-Common Software Libraries Used, by Programming Language

Programming Language	Libraries
Go	davecgh/go-spew, golang/protobuf, pkg/errors, pmezard/go-difflib, stretchr/testify, x/crypto, x/net, x/sys, x/text, yaml.v2
Java	commons-codec, commons-logging, guava, jackson-annotations, jackson-core, jacksondatabind, slf4j-api, spring-beans, spring-context, spring-expression
JavaScript	core-util-is, debug, inherits, isarray, lodash, minimist, ms, once, safe-buffer, wrappy
.NET	MS.codeanalysis.csharp, MS.ext.dependencyinjection.abstractions, MS.ext.logging.abstractions, MS.ext.primitives, MS.web.infrastructure, newtonsoft.json, sys.collections.immutable, sys.identitymodel.tokens.jwt, sys.runtime.compilerservices.unsafe, sys.text.encoding.codepages
PHP	diff, instantiator, log, php-code-coverage, php-file-iterator, php-text-template, php-timer, phptoken-stream, phpunit, version
Python	certify, chardet, idna, markupsafe, python_dateutil, pytz, requests, setuptools, six, urllib3
Ruby	activesupport, addressable, i18n, json, minitest, multi_json, rack, rake, thor, tzinfo
Swift	AFNetworking, CocoaLumberjack, Crashlytics, Fabric, FirebaseAnalyticds, FirebaseCore, FirebaseInstanceID, nanopb, PubNub, SwiftLint

SOURCE: Veracode and Cyentia Institute, 2020.

Using a "risk funnel"[8] approach to each of the languages, Veracode and Cyentia identified PHP as a risky outlier in terms of the proportion of scanned libraries that included flaws, the relatively high rate of especially exploitable and impactful flaws found, and the proportion of flaws that had published proof-of-concept exploits. Java also stood out as a relatively risky language in their framework according to these factors, although to a significantly smaller degree than PHP.

This risk funnel is associated primarily with the exploitability of code in the libraries, but there are other vulnerabilities related to the management and stability of the FOSS ecosystem. Both the Veracode/Cyentia and CII reports emphasized the challenges resulting not just from how these libraries were used and the security flaws they included (i.e., the exploitability of code in the libraries) but also from the way the open-source software ecosystem is managed.

Therefore, next, we further examine the ownership and management of the most-common libraries identified by Veracode and Cyentia in order to better assess the implications for risk management.

Management of Software Libraries

The management of libraries in the FOSS ecosystem represents another challenge to risk management in addition to the exploitability of code within the libraries. Although the importance of this issue was identified in the Veracode/Cyentia and CII reports and the ownership was assumed to vary significantly within communities associated with each of the evaluated programming languages, the reports did not further characterize this issue or examine its implications for risk management.

Ultimately, changes to the code in any of these libraries are managed by the owner of the library and the library's community of contributors. The CII report notes that the increasing importance of individual developer account security and the persistence of legacy software in the ecosystem both create additional issues for risk management (Nagle et al., 2020). This manifests in several ways; in follow-

---

[8]   In which progressive assessment of each of the factors leads to a clearer picture of the full risk from a given library or language. Although the concept of the risk funnel is not a new one, we first heard it used in this context in a discussion with a representative of Cyentia.

up discussions, we identified two significant examples: abandonware and software fragility. *Abandonware* is a term for libraries managed by individuals or small communities that, at some point, stop updating the libraries. These libraries, which, in some instances, are highly prevalent in the ecosystem, then represent a security risk as they continue to be widely used but cease to receive regular security updates. We use *software fragility* to refer to the capability of owners or contributors of a highly used library to make incompatible changes or even remove that library from the site on which it had been hosted, leading to widespread failure in applications that called that library as a dependency.

We assessed the characteristics of the owners and contributor communities for the ten most-common libraries in each of the eight languages identified by Veracode and Cyentia. This was achieved primarily by documenting the publicly available information on each of these libraries on GitHub. We searched for each library on GitHub and recorded available characteristics of the library, such as owner, owner type, organization, and nationality.

We found a wide range of values in many of these characteristics. The number of contributors to a library ranged from two to 4,280 users. Some owners were communities of developers that owned only a single library, while one user individually managed 764 libraries, and another four-member community owned 954 libraries. Some libraries had as few as two dependent libraries, while another called 2,775 as dependencies. Interestingly, we identified at least two instances of a library that had become abandonware: the php-token-stream library and the Go library go-difflib.

Although there might be valuable insights to be gained from a more in-depth analysis of some of these other characteristics, informed by our analysis and the lessons learned in the Veracode/Cyentia and CII reports, we assessed that the *ownership type* and *owner nationality* would have the most-straightforward risk-management implications for the FOSS ecosystem. We show the results in these two categories in Table 2.3 for each of the eight listed programming languages (this represents our second list of potentially risky software or businesses).

We identified three different types of owner: individual, community, and business. Of the 80 libraries examined, 28 were owned by

Table 2.3
Ownership of the Ten Most Commonly Used Libraries, by Programming Language

Language	Ownership Type			Ownership Nationality		
	Individual	Community	Business	U.S.	Non-U.S.	Unknown
Go	2	8	0	8	0	2
Java	0	0	10	9	1	0
JavaScript	6	2	2	6	1	3
.NET	1	0	9	9	1	0
PHP	9	1	0	0	8	2
Python	5	2	3	6	1	3
Ruby	4	5	1	4	4	2
Swift	1	2	7	6	2	2
Total	28 (35%)	20 (25%)	32 (40%)	48 (60%)	18 (22.5%)	14 (17.5%)

individuals, 20 by communities, and 32 by businesses. Among these owners, 48 were categorized as U.S.-based owners, 18 as non-U.S., and 14 as unknown. In addition, we also note several outliers and language-level insights:

- Eight of the ten most–commonly used PHP libraries are owned and managed by the same non–U.S.-based individual.
- Seven of the ten most–commonly used Go libraries are owned and managed by the Go Project community.
- Nine of the .NET libraries are owned by Microsoft and not hosted on GitHub.
- The Apache Software Foundation has an outsize influence in the most–commonly used libraries in Java, with 900 visible members and 2,100 hosted libraries.

Discussion

FOSS is becoming an increasingly significant aspect of critical infrastructure, and risk-management strategies are needed to address this reality. Actual prevalence estimates vary, but it is becoming clear that most modern, commercial applications are dependent on FOSS in some way, and risks associated with FOSS will need to be assessed and managed in some way as part of critical infrastructure protection. Many libraries are highly prevalent in surveyed applications, and disruptions caused by these libraries could have far-reaching consequences and varied potential impact.

Disruptions could be due to exploited flaws in the code of the libraries or due to the security and management of the libraries themselves. The analyses by CII and by Veracode and Cyentia reveal the degree to which libraries that contain known vulnerabilities are frequently integrated, often in a manner that could dramatically expand the attack surface of an application in ways that can be difficult to assess and manage. The risk of malicious actors compromising individual developer accounts or bypassing security to insert malicious code or back doors into widely used libraries is nontrivial, especially given the prevalence of libraries owned and managed by individuals, who might not have the kind of institutional security practices a larger organization might emphasize. Moreover, even when owner accounts are not compromised, poor management or capricious actions by the owners could result in widespread disruptions, such as with the examples of abandonware or "dehosting" of highly used libraries.

Together, these circumstances present a challenging aspect of the problem of critical IT risk management. In key ways, this is associated with a long-standing discussion around the benefits and drawbacks of centralization for risk management. The landscape of FOSS library owners is fragmented, with many different owner types managing libraries that are sometimes individually called as dependencies in millions of other libraries and applications. In some cases (e.g., PHP), a single individual might manage many critical libraries, creating the risk of significant disruption from careless actions or poor security practices by one person. At the same time, in some languages (e.g., Java and .NET), corporations are creating developer communities around libraries they manage, and this centralizes the landscape to some degree around one or a few entities. This could reduce risk due to assumed better security practices in such established institutions (which might also fear liability for costs of disruptions) and reduce the likelihood of key libraries being abandoned or disruptively dehosted. It might also increase risk, however, by centralizing it around a single, potentially high-value target.

Separate strategies for convening and engaging might be needed for individuals, communities, and businesses. Some critical infrastructure sectors might be more dependent on FOSS libraries in specific programming languages, and risk-mitigation strategies might need to further vary according to the ownership profile among those libraries or applications. In some cases, no clear risk-mitigation measures might be available at all, such as when the responsible parties reside outside the United States.

CHAPTER THREE

Business Risk

Next, we consider a top-down analysis of the risk posed at the vendor or company/firm level. First, we considered the economic losses that might be incurred following disruptive events and that certain small firms might be too interconnected, rather than too big, to fail. In alignment with the National Infrastructure Simulation and Analysis Center focus on systemically important critical infrastructure, certain firms might have systems of systems reliant on their solutions, although the firms themselves might be of modest size and not immediately recognizable as potentially important to critical infrastructure.

Finally, we consider whether certain firms can be reasonably mapped to specific capabilities and assets associated with NCFs. Using market analyses, we mapped firms to categories using a well-known software taxonomy. Then, using expert panels, we mapped those categories to specific NCFs.

Economic Loss and Interconnectedness

Businesses have dependency relationships with software, much as they have dependency relationships with supply chains. The U.S. Securities and Exchange Commission's Statement of Financial Accounting Standards 131 states that every firm must report key customers and suppliers that make up more than 10 percent of its sales or inputs (Barrot and Sauvagnat, 2016). Welburn et al. used this accounting standard to build a data set of approximately 6,000 publicly traded firms and the relationships between them, resulting in a network of approximately 20,000 known firm-to-firm connections (Welburn, Strong, Nekoul, et al., 2020). Given that Standard 131 requires only that a firm reveal relationships that make up at least 10 percent of its inputs or sales, many of the true linkages between firms will be unobserved. Therefore, Welburn et al. estimated the missing links using statistical methods based on a sector-to-sector gravity model (Welburn, Strong, Nekoul, et al., 2020). Specifically, a set of indicator variables for each sector-to-sector pair, together with firms' total revenue, was regressed on whether a connection between two firms was observed, thus allowing the identification of approximately 95,000 potential connections, along with the associated probability that a connection exists.

In addition to not having the full network, one unknown is the size of the connection (as measured by total sales) between any two firms. Therefore, a drawing of a network based on the probability of observing a connection is constructed, producing a directed-network graph. This directed network is augmented to create a weighted directed network. Because not all firms were represented in the network, this augmentation was done by constructing a new firm that was the aggregate of final demand and unobserved inputs to other firms, and final demand and input demand ware not directly observed. The underlying approach for estimating the weights was to develop a linear program to minimize the size of the unobserved final demand and inputs across all firms. Welburn et al. relied on knowing not only the total revenue but also the cost of goods sold. Because of the computational complexity, the analysis was limited to the largest 1,000 firms, by revenue.

From this calibration, a firm-level input/output model enabled Welburn et al. to shock firms in terms of reduction in revenue, thereby estimating two key output responses: *total economic loss* and *interconnectedness* (Welburn, Strong, Nekoul, et al., 2020). Total economic loss would be a measure of the total exposure of the economy based on a shock to an individual firm, and it captures the magnitude of an impact that an individual firm has on society. Importantly, this is correlated with the size of the firm because firms of generally the same size are likely to have about the same magnitude of impact or disruption.

Additionally, there might also be a concern with the magnitude of the external effect that a firm has on the rest of the economy relative to the firm's size as measured by the magnitude of loss from a cyberincident. By normalizing the economic loss by the firm's revenue, we controlled for the scale effect while leaving the interconnectedness, or network, effect. This generated a (unitless) multiplier factor for how the firm's network multiplied the shock. For firms with larger multipliers, shocks to those firms created ripple effects that were larger than those of firms with smaller multipliers. Although these are just two measures that could be used, they provide scale and interconnectedness measures that alternative policy interventions might aim to control. In effect, we examined whether firms were not just too *big* to fail but whether they were also too *interconnected* to fail.

As the first step, given a 1-percent drop in revenue for all firms, the model captures the direct economic loss incurred by each firm. However, as firms are shocked, not only do they lose revenue; their customers and suppliers lose revenue because of sales lost to the firm directly and reductions in inputs necessary for production. That is, there is both an upstream and downstream supply-chain impact. Thus, it is not only the size of a firm that becomes relevant but also its interconnectedness to other firms in the supply chain and their sizes.

Second, because firms differ in size, the loss multiplier of each firm was calculated by normalizing the economic loss by the firm's revenue, which produces a metric that is independent of company size but captures the degree of interconnectedness that each firm exhibits with other firms.

Using the methods outlined in Welburn, Strong, Nekoul, et al., 2020, we list the ten technology and communication sector firms (i.e., companies that generally fall under the Connect NCF category, although some also provide computing and enterprise software).[1] First, Table 3.1 lists the ten firms with the greatest total economic loss (i.e., loss to the given firm, as well as its supply chain) that would result from a 1-percent shock (loss of revenue) to the firm.

Unsurprisingly, the top firms are large but not necessarily in terms of revenue. Importantly, they represent firms that are large *and*

---

[1]   These correspond to North American Industry Classification System sectors 541 and 517. We believe that these two sectors best represent firms in IT business and services.

Table 3.1
Ten Information and Communication
Technology Firms with the Greatest
Potential Economic Loss

Firm	Sector
Amazon	Tech
Comcast	Communication
Apple	Tech
AT&T	Communication
IBM	Tech
Tech Data	Tech
Alphabet	Tech
Cisco Systems	Tech
Microsoft	Tech
Dell Technologies	Tech

SOURCE: Welburn, Strong, Nekoul, et al., 2020.

have substantial relationships with other firms. It is this combination of characteristics that causes these firms to suffer the greatest economic impact. Next, Table 3.2 reproduces the ten most-*interconnected* firms (together, Tables 3.1 and 3.2 represent the third list of potentially risky software or businesses).

As discussed earlier, these are not the largest firms by revenue. For example, GoDaddy enjoyed revenue of approximately $2 billion in 2018 but has an estimated loss multiplier of approximately 180, suggesting that, if GoDaddy were to suffer a shock of $1 million, there would be an estimated economic loss of approximately $180 million, owing to how many firms rely on GoDaddy. In contrast, Amazon enjoyed revenue of approximately $280 billion in 2018 but has a loss multiplier of only 5.4. Although a 1-percent disruption to Amazon would be costlier in terms of total economic loss than a 1-percent disruption to GoDaddy, GoDaddy appears to punch above its weight in terms of disrupting other firms.

Table 3.2
The Ten Most Interconnected Firms

Firm	Sector
GoDaddy	Tech
Workday	Tech
Diebold Nixdorf	Tech
Verisk Analytics	Tech
National Cash Register	Tech
Motorola Solutions	Tech
Computer Discount Warehouse	Tech
DISH Network	Communication
Arrow Electronics	Tech
Securities Software and Consulting Technologies Holdings	Tech

SOURCE: Welburn, Strong, Nekoul, et al., 2020.

Discussion

There is an important trade-off when considering policy interventions that target the largest firms (in terms of economic loss) versus targeting the most-interconnected firms, as measured by the loss multiplier. If the goal is to reduce the size of economic loss, targeting those with the largest amount of economic loss should be considered. By focusing on only the large firms, we might ignore moderate but incredibly interconnected firms that could cause a large cascading failure that would affect many firms but by potentially a smaller amount. Knowing that firms exist that might be too interconnected to fail means that we cannot focus solely on the firms with the largest amounts of economic loss.

Although this portion of the analysis has incorporated the impact of a disruption, it does not incorporate the probability that a disruption will take place or the scale of the disruption. As a result, it does not take into account the full concept of risk.

Mapping National Critical Functions to Businesses

In this section, we provide an alternative method of identifying companies that provide critical services to the U.S. economy. As mentioned, the NCF effort provides a list of capabilities that are deemed critical to the United States. Subsequent work within DHS led to the decomposition of the statements within certain NCFs that identified specific assets (e.g., Provide DNS [Domain Name System] Software within the Supply NCF category). However, to the best of our knowledge, there has been no rigorous effort to connect these functions to actual companies that provide those services. Therefore, in this section, we attempt to develop those associations.

First, we posit that, if we could reasonably and systematically identify the kinds of software that are used to support a given NCF, we could then identify software companies that develop those applications, as shown in Figure 3.1.

Figure 3.1
Mapping National Critical Functions to Firms Through a Software Taxonomy

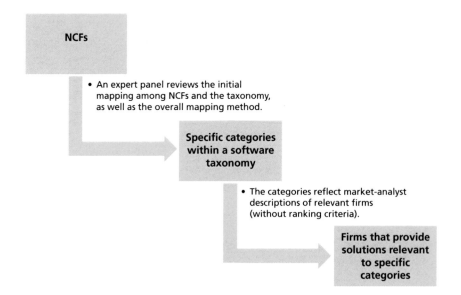

This process is composed of two main steps:

1. Map NCFs to an appropriate software taxonomy.
2. Map those software categories to firms that manufacture that software.

We describe each of these steps in more detail below.

Mapping National Critical Functions to a Software Taxonomy

To better assess the types of critical IT products and the risks associated with them, we required a proven software taxonomy that would facilitate characterizing broad groups of software products, assessing their importance to the NCFs, and identifying the risks that might be associated with them. This top-down approach allowed a much wider characterization and risk assessment across the landscape of products and software than we would have by attempting to assess many individual examples.

We searched for publicly available documentation on efforts to create software classification systems or taxonomies to guide our analysis. We assessed multiple sources to inform our analysis, including

- the Association for Computing Machinery's Computing Classification System (see Association for Computing Machinery, undated)
- International Data Corporation's Worldwide Software Taxonomy report (Morris, 2017)
- the International Foundation for Information Technology's taxonomy (see International Foundation for Information Technology, undated)
- the WAND IT taxonomy (see WAND, undated)
- the Corporate Executive Board (now Gartner) Chief Information Officer Council IT Services Taxonomy (Corporate Executive Board, 2015).

For the purpose of this research, we used a modified version of the International Data Corporation's Worldwide Software Taxonomy (Morris,

2017) because it offered the most exhaustive and mutually exclusive classification of business software categories, simply described, and employed a hierarchical categorization structure.

Once we had identified a suitable software taxonomy, we mapped software categories that were likely to be related in a meaningful way to a select group of the NCFs. Because this exercise relies solely on expertise and judgment, we convened an expert panel to review the approach and discuss specific mapping decisions.

Certain NCFs are defined at a high level (e.g., Enforce Law in the Manage category), for which it would be difficult to bound the IT solutions that support them. For this approach, we selected NCFs that have been described in some detail (e.g., Provide IT Products and Services in the Supply category) given prior DHS analysis that provided a breakout of 11 subelements and assets associated with this function (DHS, 2009):

- Produce and provide networking elements.
- Produce and provide security and policy compliance elements.
- Produce and provide operation system services software.
- Produce and provide business operations, database, and business intelligence software and services.
- Produce and provide managed network and data center elements.
- Produce and provide semiconductors.
- Produce and provide storage hardware, software, and services.
- Provide life-cycle product and service integrity, certification, and other assurance functions and mechanisms.
- Develop DNS software.
- Develop and provide secure appliances that support DNS.
- Produce and provide control system products, supervisory control and data acquisition (SCADA), and other automation systems.

Mapping Software Categories to Firms
This second step is achieved by reviewing industry analyst reports for each of these categories, which are defined at a level that roughly matches software market segments. We use these analyst reports to develop a list of firms that provide solutions for that market segment and

software category. We did not adopt any prioritization logic from these analyst reports because each seeks to highlight its own rationale, from market share to customer feedback. This task was simply to enumerate the firms themselves. Any prioritization thereafter should be determined with regard to critical infrastructure and likely consequences.

Therefore, with this framework, the firms related to the subelement "Produce and provide control system products, SCADA, and other automation systems" within the Provide IT Products and Services NCF (in the Supply category) are shown in Table 3.3 (this represents our fourth list of potentially risky software or businesses).

Discussion

Connecting specific firms to NCFs is a top-down approach to identifying critical IT services and businesses. To illustrate the method of analysis, we defined specific NCF capabilities at a level at which an experienced technical expert can identify categories of software that likely support the critical function. Although the work described herein proves fairly straightforward for certain categories of NCFs; many others will require analyses that either decompose the function to this same level or provide a deeper dive into specific verticals of the software market.

The results from this effort can be used in a number of ways. First, one potentially interesting observation involves foreign-owned,

Table 3.3
Industrial Control System Firms

Firm Category	Firm
SCADA systems	Applied Control Engineering, General Electric, Rockwell Automation, Schneider Electric, Siemens
Advanced distribution management systems	Axxiom, Electrical Transient and Analysis Program (ETAP), General Electric, H3C, Hewlett Packard, Hitachi, Indra, Minsait Advanced Control Systems, Oracle, OSI Hardware, Schneider Electric, Siemens, Survalent Technology
Manufacturing execution systems	Aptean; AVEVA; Dassault Systèmes; Emerson; Epicor; FORCAM; General Electric; Honeywell; iBASEt; iTAC Software; Leading2Lean; MPDV; Oracle; Parsec; Rockwell Automation; Sepasoft; Siemens; Systems, Applications, and Products in Data Processing (SAP); Werum IT Solutions

-controlled, or -influenced software manufacturing firms. To the extent that this becomes an issue (i.e., identifying an NCF that is supported by foreign-owned, -controlled, or -influenced firms), the methodology provided here might assist in identifying such firms. Further, as we map firms to software categories, and thereafter to NCFs, we might discover firms that have a larger footprint among multiple NCFs, potentially identifying these firms as priority companies on which to focus cybersecurity resilience efforts.

CHAPTER FOUR

Conclusion

Understanding and defining the riskiest IT products and services are complicated processes because there is no single, authoritative way of assessing risk, suggesting that there will be multiple ways to describe it. Consequently, this research takes four approaches to understanding the problem of critical IT products and services, each producing its own insights. Given the unbounded nature of the problem, we first sought to better understand the state of what is possible, both in terms of data availability and analytical modeling of risk, then to provide useful, actionable results for DHS. Where possible, we attempted to be data driven, although we recognize that no single data source or framework will provide a complete solution. Further, in cases in which we were not able to justify inferences of risk, we identified properties that we believed would be strongly correlated with risk.

The four approaches were as follows:

- First, we identified and integrated many disparate data sources, in order to identify the most-severe vulnerabilities that have a high likelihood of exploitation and software applications within the U.S. internet protocol space.
- Next, given the emerging software ecosystem embedded within modern, commercial applications, we collected original data in order to map out the software dependency and ownership structure of the most-referenced libraries.
- We also leveraged existing work to identify specific IT and communication companies that had the greatest measure of business

interconnectedness and could potentially suffer the greatest economic loss.

- Finally, we developed an original technique for linking NCFs to actual software companies supporting those functions.

Although we believe that these approaches are appropriate and reasonable, we also recognize that they and their accompanying results provide only a first step because there will inevitably be other factors that federal policymakers will want (and need) to consider when taking action.

From each line of effort, we drew insight and found the following:

- First, a better understanding of software vulnerabilities requires additional contextual information about the vulnerabilities that exist in which industries and companies and how those applications support a firm and its operations. Further, identification of these riskiest vulnerabilities might require that policymakers address the software manufacturer (to notify them of new vulnerabilities) or engage the company running the vulnerable software (and convince it to update or upgrade its systems). Finally, any particular list of software and application vulnerabilities can change quickly with time, either because of software updates or because of evolving threats and attacker motives.
- Second, we identified how commercial applications, to a significant degree, are built on small, distributed FOSS libraries owned and maintained by a variety of user types. Risk assessment can no longer be based simply on application-level analysis because applications (especially web applications) are built on these collections of libraries that have their own risk profiles. Moreover, the landscape of these libraries is constantly changing as libraries are added and updated frequently, and it might be challenging to quickly assess the way in which that landscape is changing and what those changes imply for risk mitigation. DHS therefore needs a new way to think about software risk assessment that incorporates the risk from open-source software dependencies into a broader software risk framework.

- Third, in regard to economic loss and interdependency, the results provide an objective method for identifying potential impacts due to business supply chains for publicly traded companies within the IT and communication sectors (i.e., those generally within the Connect NCF category). These results, we argue, provide an additional perspective into identifying potential gaps that the National Risk Management Center might have when assessing the most-critical companies. However, although they provide measures of impact and interdependency, inferring more-relevant issues of business risk will require additional research.
- Finally, for mapping NCFs to software companies, we developed a method for leveraging market analyses to identify firms relevant to specific software market segments. The expert judgment required to map software market segments to certain NCFs is straightforward for some NCFs, but, for other NCFs (many in the Manage NCF category), there is insufficient granularity to pursue this approach. Nevertheless, for specific areas that might be of high interest to critical infrastructure analysts (e.g., SCADA, security compliance software, network routing), this work allowed us to develop first-order—unprioritized—lists of firms with solutions relevant to several NCFs.

References

Association for Computing Machinery, "ACM Computing Classification System," undated. As of October 28, 2020:
https://dl.acm.org/ccs

Barrot, Jean-Noël, and Julien Sauvagnat, "Input Specificity and the Propagation of Idiosyncratic Shocks in Production Networks," *Quarterly Journal of Economics*, Vol. 131, No. 3, August 2016, pp. 1543–1592.

CISA—*See* Cybersecurity and Infrastructure Security Agency.

Common Platform Enumeration, homepage, last updated November 28, 2014. As of January 14, 2021:
https://cpe.mitre.org/

Corporate Executive Board, "CIO Council IT Services Taxonomy," briefing slides obtained by the authors, 2015.

CPE—*See* Common Platform Enumeration.

Cybersecurity and Infrastructure Security Agency, "National Critical Functions," webpage, undated. As of October 28, 2020:
https://www.cisa.gov/national-critical-functions

———, "Vulnerability Remediation Requirements for Internet-Accessible Systems," U.S. Department of Homeland Security Binding Operational Directive 19-02, April 29, 2019. As of January 14, 2021:
https://cyber.dhs.gov/bod/19-02/

DHS—*See* U.S. Department of Homeland Security.

FIRST—*See* Forum of Incident Response and Security Teams.

Forum of Incident Response and Security Teams, "Common Vulnerability Scoring System SIG," webpage, undated a. As of October 28, 2020:
https://www.first.org/cvss/

————, "Exploit Prediction Scoring System (EPSS)," webpage, undated b. As of October 28, 2020:
https://www.first.org/epss/

International Foundation for Information Technology, "Taxonomy of Key Management Software Types or Categorizations," webpage, undated. As of October 28, 2020:
https://www.if4it.com/SYNTHESIZED/FRAMEWORKS/TAXONOMY/management_software_taxonomy.html

Morris, Henry D., *IDC's Worldwide Software Taxonomy, 2017*, Framingham, Mass.: International Data Corporation, August 2017.

Nagle, Frank, Jessica Wilkerson, James Dana, and Jennifer L. Hoffman, *Vulnerabilities in the Core: Preliminary Report and Census II of Open Source Software*, Linux Foundation, Core Infrastructure Initiative, and Laboratory for Innovation Science at Harvard, February 2020. As of January 14, 2021:
https://www.coreinfrastructure.org/programs/census-program-ii/

National Institute of Standards and Technology, U.S. Department of Commerce, "National Vulnerability Database," webpage, undated. As of October 28, 2020:
https://nvd.nist.gov/

National Telecommunications and Information Administration, "Software Bill of Materials," webpage, undated. As of October 20, 2020:
https://www.ntia.gov/SBOM

NIST—*See* National Institute of Standards and Technology.

Obama, Barack, "Executive Order 13636 of February 12, 2013: Improving Critical Infrastructure Cybersecurity," *Federal Register*, Vol. 78, No. 33, February 19, 2013, pp. 11739–11744. As of January 14, 2021:
https://www.federalregister.gov/documents/2013/02/19/2013-03915/improving-critical-infrastructure-cybersecurity

Public Law 107-296, Homeland Security Act of 2002, November 25, 2002. As of May 12, 2019:
https://www.govinfo.gov/app/details/PLAW-107publ296

Sonatype, *2019 State of the Software Supply Chain*, undated.

Souppaya, Murugiah P., and Karen Scarfone, *Guide to Enterprise Patch Management Technologies*, Gaithersburg, Md.: U.S. Department of Commerce, National Institute of Standards and Technology, Special Publication 800-40, Rev. 3, July 22, 2013. As of January 14, 2021:
https://www.nist.gov/publications/guide-enterprise-patch-management-technologies

Trump, Donald, "Executive Order 13800 of May 11, 2017: Strengthening the Cybersecurity of Federal Networks and Critical Infrastructure," *Federal Register,* Vol. 82, No. 93, May 16, 2017, pp. 22391–22397. As of January 14, 2021:
https://www.federalregister.gov/documents/2017/05/16/2017-10004/strengthening-the-cybersecurity-of-federal-networks-and-critical-infrastructure

U.S. Code, Title 6, Domestic Security; Chapter 1, Homeland Security Organization; Subchapter III, Science and Technology in Support of Homeland Security; Section 185, Federally Funded Research and Development Centers. As of March 20, 2021:
https://uscode.house.gov/
view.xhtml?req=(title:6%20section:185%20edition:prelim)

U.S. Computer Emergency Readiness Team, "Alerts," undated a. As of January 14, 2021:
https://us-cert.cisa.gov/ncas/alerts

———, "National Cyber Awareness System," undated b. As of January 14, 2021:
https://us-cert.cisa.gov/ncas

U.S. Department of Homeland Security, *Information Technology Sector Baseline Risk Assessment,* Washington, D.C., August 2009. As of October 28, 2020:
https://www.dhs.gov/xlibrary/assets/nipp_it_baseline_risk_assessment.pdf

Veracode and Cyentia Institute, "State of Software Security: Open Source Edition," May 19, 2020. As of October 19, 2020:
https://library.cyentia.com/report/report_003621.html

"Vulnerabilities Equities Policy and Process for the United States Government," November 15, 2017. As of April 28, 2021:
https://trumpwhitehouse.archives.gov/sites/whitehouse.gov/files/images/External%20-%20Unclassified%20VEP%20Charter%20FINAL.PDF

WAND, "WAND Information Technology Taxonomy," webpage, undated. As of October 28, 2020:
https://www.wandinc.com/wand-information-technology-taxonomy

Welburn, Jonathan William, and Aaron M. Strong, "Systemic Cyber Risk and Aggregate Impacts," *Risk Analysis,* February 16, 2021.

Welburn, Jonathan William, Aaron Strong, Florentine Eloundou Nekoul, Justin Grana, Krystyna Marcinek, Osonde A. Osoba, Nirabh Koirala, and Claude Messan Setodji, *Systemic Risk in the Broad Economy: Interfirm Networks and Shocks in the U.S. Economy,* Santa Monica, Calif.: RAND Corporation, RR-4185-RC, 2020. As of October 26, 2020:
https://www.rand.org/pubs/research_reports/RR4185.html